JOHN WILKINSON

RECKITT'S BLUE

LONDON NEW YORK CALCUTTA

Seagull Books, 2012

© John Wilkinson, 2012

ISBN-13   978 0 8574 2 092 3

British Library Cataloguing-in-Publication Data
A catalogue record for this book is available from the British Library

Typeset in Arno Pro by Seagull Books, Calcutta, India
Printed and bound by Hyam Enterprises, Calcutta, India

RECKITT'S BLUE

CONTENTS

The Swing   1

    What Gives   37

    Tornada   51

Reckitt's Blue   61

    Roundabout   93

THE SWING

Heads of the characters hammer through daisies

I

Conifers
drop packets on the pool that receiving,
wrinkles. Something shrunk back
to water's edge.
                    It trembles
like a compass. Petals piece their coronal
and daylight's moth dips, it does or did
compel a certain hierarchy,
starting point where seeds crackle,
            peppered over water.

Tawny stops
rise joyfully, descend to view themselves
descend, as though one dress
of glass labels shook its consignment off,
            cleared,
collected what it needed
to shake again, and took the fall.
            How can
light be wrung out of its milk set.
                    Discursive star,
withdraw so as to shine?

Postulants
receiving fronds, stroke ruffled water,
as if shipped oars lower.
A bough eases.
            Grass sinks with seed.
Activities
may yet advance, but on a highland strip
emissaries from flat countries,
fouled in light, twitch
            like stop-go pond insects.
Grass postpones unloading.

II

Seeing as
our eyes are mounted, eyes protrude,
the floor can be listened out for.
What's heard in its rodomontade
           sculpts our ears
as though for hearing. Treetops
flourish
high above the carriers, or so their burnt
Jerusalem below-foot submits,
           bursting for next year.
Cinch up their slipperiness
with bands of birdsong,
                    hear one gleam.

Our high gleam
from shoe to shattered forms,
dances like a trilling sycamore sky does;
           its multitudinousness
air lost grip of. I recall
cress fringing chalk-white water,
plinth and clasp to broken
porch, careened step:
from an invisible factor
wanly radiant, seeped out what prolifically

was churned up,
frothed and whipped, now an arc sur-
bates on them, a heel balks,
the shoe's truthful curve touches earth,
                    it binds
but is not bound itself,
           brought low or chamfered off:
a tight bracelet chokes the sapling
forced to exuberance.
Ours, I thought.

Moreover: if—
seeing husks buoyed among the interlace,
if it gleams an eye bulges.

III

Come to that,
what light should any take to heart,
      not to feel too pumped up?
The burnish stretched—
      who could once foresee it,
what stared round in its so-high manner
icing the entire span,
      surfacing with spicules,
wanted to give birth,
lick its recipient into shape,
      then it bounded fitfully,
through its fluttering it seemed I walked
eager for more stuff.

No telling
fronds amorphous held in suspense,
telling them to swing loose.
      The pang hangs at hand, but
jerks soggily, not defined either. Should I
      take the pang to heart,
the scale of it, the
image in full view that won't touch
but looms perennially?—
I know who I am by how I respond.
Then feel a strong temptation to pluck.
      Leave off, my love, leave

this window,
      stretch yourself more freely.
The starvelings' eyes are ice-encrusted,
new-born struggle.
To hold our own, then give it
      like clean water,
shape it glancingly:
To take issue, give as good

    like vaccine,
what we'd got gripped:
        engineered, the shadows
hanker for their providential steel bridge,
retrospectively, keel their tangent space.

IV

Jenny Wren,
all mostly spied before a straw had fallen
which way it would fall, it did
                    directly flutter.
Eyes fleck, eyes get foxed, eyes start
back, I start, I start, I start
behind the cascade, but it was smoke,
not the mist
happening on first blush. You jingle
like a bracelet, I can't still you only make
                    you out high-pitched,
a maddened buzz between fingers.

Right behind,
Kit, tend the fire behind the rattan screen.
The grid seemed to control flicker,
                    not so—
numbers spool like blinds and bobbins
to their red bed.
                Construing embers
will not reconstruct smoke, will not post-
form, eyes freeze, eyes blank in alabaster,
                    fail, fail, follow.
For all that, smoke does remain,
chuffed across sky that might have been.

Jenny Wren,
your bolster is firmed up with newsprint,
even the hard bolster
                smokes from a deep internal
rot, rot is fire, the smoulder
                    smothered in its own fuel.
Who can see what falls
if her ear is clamped to numbers,

if her eye appears as a board's weak point,
    befalling
underneath her own sheltering form?
Someone was minded to specify
a subset,
        fluctuate and disperse.

V

Rain combs thatch,
benches angle, then we watch the dished
ghostly images fan out,
   blink in their after-image
declination, sink below their dotted line,
slip down the streets,
      these are secret
stations of our tribe, these are riders
on the bundle, on the big thunder packet,
these are one thing, as such,
even as they flap their pinions
   above the settles.

     Ceaseless rain
shrinks windows round my sister,
ghosts thicken, gaining weight
within a long-endured house. These were
watched into permanence, into
forms each attains, couldn't
   summarily resign,
nor outside their long house alter state,
sort, though each frequent its hollow:
water churns, water shrinks, water laps,
   solidifies,

water dis-
torts—even if the drupe bursts,
inside the crease sticks a mauve dust
   like inside a knee or elbow.
Spring dissenting almost stops. We will
snap to their emerging
guideline, so help them,
   they were meant
in their Pythagorean harness, to ride forth.

Promoter! you came in just before
the golden side flips up, shines brightly,
                    engulfs the globe.

VI

I balloon.
You clap. No let can be admitted.
Set pieces wobbling in their cradle,
loosened. Tracked
by the casings cracked open then ejected,
far from their barrel slugs flew,
             silver lenses dilate
against the barn. Magpies and jays
hang, birds from every sighted slug
             start to bloat,
their outward glossiness
harbouring a cartridge of maggots,
squirming shot.

             Now dismount.
Here a breath bursts
out of tilted fault blocks, staining stone.
             But no more of that . . .
none of that loose travel, have no trade
with fault-tolerance, or truck with
turbulence or moult.
             Feathered grass
jimmying the crannies,
philodendron making light of heaps,
I set the aperture, or is it
climbing rose, or is it capillary force . . .

hence measure
set hyperbolic would become the lever,
seed-heads whirl so fast they
             set earth to cellulate
chunks of rock, the ore scallops,
globes of ice break in geodesic spray,
             shone-up fronds
canopy above us, and the slapdash ones

wriggling in their cracks, were a product
of our watch,
cleft commensals, the seethers stuck.

VII

Open wide.
Vapour interjects through vapour.
Flights of larks trill on the sparse
bridge of coir,
bridge of multi-core. Predatory
thinkpad:
        if I salute I flake, if I flake I flutter
gaping underneath, hung low, activated
by one twitching floater, one spinner,
                most
feck not smaller than a universe entire
pearled when a fly tickles my dead
centre aspect—how

do clouds work,
like a struggling fly capitulates
while at base the homing signal flashes,
dimpling a high-impact panel.
        A signal
billows, affines on the manifold
tack, tack, tack, an exponential
map transits to the left while red alert
is triggered by another set at odds.
Waterboatmen, grubs,
blink in parallel,

rack sunsets.
Swag palls of flies pixelate the spirit
overheads, infurling vapour
breathes and I respond to (as is).
I consist in supernumerary droplets.
I consist against a biting flower.
        Synchronise,
drag outward-going festoon.
              Moreover

clouds resolve above mosquitoes,
unload. Above cloud
a meteor shower wakes a deep afterglow.

THE BEACONS

Birds touching bills deploy as emissaries of those
tribunes from another city, they will be consoled as
night breaks over night, caught up as does any straw
made much of on a mountaintop, bear weight.
Bent lines below continue in their work of heaping.

Up above is rustle,
squawk, chatter.
Much made on top
behind the cascade
flashes to its neighbour citadel.

The cities will unite while the lines always trudge.
Gashed, gnashed, throat moshing at its mouthpiece,
birdsong drives forward in a pentatonic cascade,
tongue to tunnel tongue, the descendant
looping through vowels sinks rapidly into a swallet.

The fleeting house hauls through darkly comic dust.
The dam of shadows carried one by one,
set down at the end of every line, heaps a dam of
shadow hods, the grain sacks ruined, saturated
in a cloudburst, profligate they sprout, ramp them.

Wings harden air.
Squabbling and wild
aggravation thrive,
but they shriek
in consonance and their wing-blades semaphore. Earth
gurgles sullenly through springs then springs forth.

AT A LOSS

A character frets out what he seeks but to disavow
as if openly,
thinks to put more value on what's spilt,
          so the once-spurned will accost,
as he sees, as he is bound then to own, both
profess and embrace—
standing out importunate against
claggy backcloth, feathered bindings, head-dresses,
knots of feathers, feather coats, rooms
choked with pin-feathers, pages and a
queue of output,
          will accost the spitting character:
                    less so would the crest
that seemed to surmount the helm
          take renouncing, submit to such forfeiture,
still the plume nods as on a colonial governor's
pith helmet in times past,
still the cables flex against the landing-stage, cracking
with the to and fro of arraignment and forgiveness,
expulsion and revaluing.

          Moreover,
I could disperse in such an atmosphere, this befalls
every visitor, cares lift off the
witness to its auguries unperturbed. Auguries
of what failed to follow, therefore set aside,
          mulling stars in their bowls
when icy, sampling colostrum when vapid,
auguries firm up as keen
traces of time having scarified. End points fester.
Surely the dove must have gone before the feather.
The midpoint gets massaged.
Ocean tenses along its blue tendons,
even though sentiment stays sluggish.
The artillery of the spirit coughs.

                    My character
brandishes a whisk, my son wields a camera,
snapping the illimitable fledge.
                    Hand the camera to that black boy,
he can take our picture while unearthing himself,
that's me done for,
our picture fades into a bleached rectangle,
                    the long and short of it dies.

Over the next ridge there's said to be just masses of
clean air, but with the new road the next ridge
                    has moved further off.
Wider yet the relegation zone, its scarecrow
magazines, its blank, empty dishes
stuck with feathers, can these sounding vessels
be the team we must work with?—
                    so it would appear,
the vapour trails, the phantom regiments
cease to waver and start to bring in revenue. Gun
emplacements good for a quick return,
subterranean cells for a more measured yield,
anyway, all solidifies.
Beneath the overlapping sky a haze bakes hard,
                    everything is covered, thought of,
fluctuations don't unsettle long-term prospects.
Still, an edge of moral hazard
must be viewable, even in a high gloss shot—
the firmament stacks up because
a little sweat lubricates the waves bunched
underneath, rolls them out as though a postcard
edge played to their remaining strengths
                    as a cash cow,
                    as a sea cucumber,

so too kittiwakes roister in formation,
make impenetrable the rack left behind;
their formations wheel recruiting the once-spurned,

spiffily they up-and-over, dip and roll,
                         crests, vanes, pinions, ramp
the cassowary, the flightless
            into their apotheosis,
fantastic roc that swoops, eagles
tremulous on high air,
hawks will not fail the light, their hooded
eyes don't blink,
            snatch the motor-mouth and drop
eggs earthwards, earth that has my say—
                         whatever character
will take my part and make it occupy the whole,
snacks on my voice,
            claims my fealty, passes me my cut.
This character exposes itself,
            no more than the backing
for the character who flies off from the atoll struck
from his sidereal setting, spangled sea,
cement works:

blue as it peels back exposes his churning breast—
is that the ruby an eagle swoops to carry to its eerie,
            its serrated beak
gashing to his marrow, pecking order on the quick
cured ceramic?

Muggy labyrinth and feathers intermesh.
Dusk perturbs air with feathers, much as if
beating wings understood the way they must go,
                         they migrate
I presume towards a junk shop
where everything any of us lost, has ended up,
and will lie incumbent on us, haggling over what
            at some level,
            stays with us vividly because lost,
blue braids binding each to each under pressing sky,
incumbent generally, because lost.

BLUE FLASH LIMBO

James, those are sirens, we should
go inside before the streets fold.

Alert for impetigo, sculled, ever
troop, ever under looming cloud

watchful of a thick felt, prodding
to contuse bounce or joust,

slapped and fingered round the ribs,
a stumbler asks a cally pat-hook

what in the name of goodness
should announce its figure, skk,

totter stunned steps with lank
grass or plantain leaves or kelp,

could that hostage stride and jump?
I hugged myself, feeling crushed,

heavily ironed was their stroud,
their denim, their confit crackle

sparking a full-scale alert: stacked
rats, stacked bats, too far gone

to consume or come between
we who snuck in baby-talk. Tk tk.

What gives? Niche complexity
blunders round eyes on stage,

discursive every time, knocks back
the principal bound up in itself,

squalid tailings everywhere
behind its ethical product strewn.

The indigo rush to descant muff,
wah-wahs bob like floats and kick.

VIII

As a shut
lily lifts and lowers its head,
balloons and flattens, flaps, slaps and slumps,
                    fails light
behind its hood, denies it,
            dangling like wolfbane,
tossed on the air sighs a canister
releasing what was once my voice, at
least some dispersed,
            before what might
fructify in the vault, instead clambers

clumsily,
fails light, swags of shade
overspill their pursed blue outline.
            Some unfetter vocals from their lips
but then flunk,
                    well the cap fits so I
wear it and I lost my shirt so I'll
            cop
this umbrella emblem. Subfusc.
Cirrus bars blue sky, lapped
before those spirits
well-hydrated surge across,
draped in a blue, an overhanging

pellicle,
draped in cotton folds.
What bleaching treats to such disjunct
fire puffs out shirts
with standard issue, frep linten mace,
bleached
            bird-embroched habitat,
universal. One metre takes wing above.
Best mind shirt be my hammock.

The aperture my lagging.
Surd hiss clamp. Sigh.
Masks peer out of cargo, these solicitous.

IX

Unfathomed
cavity, just a smudge
starts dispersing underneath. Shook-out
foil, anoxygenic trace, long trapped.
            How with capillaries?
Dancers maze round the plinth
below puzzled Cupid, creep out from ferny
glow rain quenches,
dreariness snags fabric so it streams
eyeful aftereffects, casts their long
shadows down a dead reef.

Long waiting
dropped its shoe; horizon riddled,
cries danced staccato over mud-flats,
            they must sound deeps
to then resound in, shot and shot
dipped and dipped like waterfowl fly under,
            though wincing at every pull
calendared against their flight—
                        pulling threads
to dislodge a cotton plug.

Cistern plug
won't degrade, the spigots seize, the man-
hole covers rust solid.
            I inverted skirl
streaming upward, coped with
loss as arrowheads of difference
rake the floodplain,
                  tidal marks
had been partnered off like tongues
meticulously jaw-matched
            could front for you in singing ropes.
But shadow worms

twist, thrash their iron basin,
underlings churn,
              a deeper, pensive throb
shakes light-bonded sand. The pores open.

X

Ghosts of combs,
ghostly
            foot-pile, sun-brinked,
crimsoning the gun-room, brood as dusk
slots between barred eyes,
crimsoning the burnt grass clearing,
nodding donkeys halt and jennies still.
            Seed-heads gleam
carborundum-like, slag heaps glint,
necks twist inquisitively,
cupids wriggle out
of horsehair settles and of daub,
many struggle free from each impress, one
            enduring prototype puffs,

setting course
from four corners, filling sails like cheeks
tack by teeth of the storm:
            Bucket wheresoe'er action is.
            Specifically expunged is.
Orphan flesh must pick their organs
bound for facial log-on.
Some fan out various types, boxed.
But then
            bite the rough with the mouth,
but then
flinch behind bars,
but then darken, then at last
            re-set into the socket,

some black eye/
a shiner
punched against the canvas, glows
            livid, glows yellow-blue
pressed against a stock-mounted sight:

strengthening it ranges, sweeps the alcoves,
probes light silos.
                        Charcoal-burners
pile smoke behind in powder-puffs
for spring decor,
            thickets rattle,
puzzle and dismay Cupid, propped above.

XI

Moreover,
drop dance
       vesicles
heedless ripple moiré. Long neg-
lected bridle-path, glebe
less frequented, even so
doesn't fade but replicates in fan-shapes.
       Lilies fester, fleur-de-lys packets,
rubbish has been gusted down there
instead of bestowed or dropped,
       handsome is as handsome
strews fly-wings, veined leaves—
for it is cormorant light pecks and pecks

saturat-
ed ruts, distorts the felloes,
wavering the spokes,
scales fall and cartridge cases stud the verge.
       Scattered lilies
stab into the soakaway,
and tossed, merged, all become . . .
Oh! if only I were a sounding vessel/
       blank blank
winked at by ostensible
through-traffic, if at my imprudent breath
flap butterflies—
no chain reaction, but fendillated light!

But feet tan-
gle in the
chained shadows, stumble in depressions,
re-pack a drovers' path,
recurse unto resolved soil.
       Pluck down I say,
pack them, pluck down

their brilliance, airy jive,
            they shall be sore beset.
The iridescent bridle path
branches and complicates:
their shields yet display the one emblem.

XII

Phantomlike
sheaves reap, leather calves. Troughs
baring barrens to their deluge, cloud that
        belly-flops
for canopy, oh if!, nylon flurries
spark in pink powder-rooms—
busts behind fine nostrils crumble,
fingers snap cuffs. Rabbit feet
brush cheeks,

                        fur
shocked, stroked and stroked, fur
hair rubs against for a centrifuge of sparks.
What costumiers' light, make-up
bare bulbs will saturate?

Pulley strap
jerking its contraption, a holster
dips down an
airy stack to stained stone,
        flushing via a
hair-lipped scuttle, via a patent
sling-back gushing throat throughout the
shower-burst,
                sodden all evacuate/
bronze drips below,
sojourners squelching in the folds
scoop a cracked cistern rather than abase
to vivid waters
        Stop wells with rubble:

let these stench,
spew, spring a leak, infuriate the wind
in its storehouses, let lightning fork to fork
force animals
to drop their young, a powder burst

           bruise canvas:
cloud rushes
by above the bursting machinery, plumping
bales up from puffs of talc, heaping
                    bales upon bales.

XIII

Clouds, leaves, swarm,
cupids do, startled green
stalks poke out and one basket tumbles open—
grain mildews, grapes rankle, loose limbs flail,
reproduced and reproducing this
pastoral set. I stare
        into the green, I stare, I stare,
violence gouges out the picture-
plain, a storm sweeps
the elevation, routs sky.
        Tricorn hat bounces.
        Ropes compel Astarte
to and fro.

Pink satin
shoe flies. In flying it suspends
cell-phone services. Voiced air swings
what the seasonal arc made out to swing.
Now when handed from the swing
you tilt your head for all
its attitude, your ruffles
won't a moment sidetrack
my glance from the pause
        button,
it's a toe-in, an inspiracy,
pointing to a back road, towards a cut hill.

Meteorites
clatter like machinery condemned,
        nearly crush,
but I missed my mark too missed my mark/
refreshed a flop bouquet, a handful
of foliage, of notes.
The amassed light was never quenched.
The brilliant embolus struck out, over-
flying conifers.

White stained a dredged estuary.
All said, her shoe
flew like a no-show morning star, it
          showed an empty hand
for what it holds.

XIV

The door breaks
open then the door breaks open.
   High shoe tilts, its afterglow,
its trail rasped and scrubbed.
Wresting it away her lovers
     hooked and eyed
round the ankle-strap,
sensed emptiness's lineaments,
tore apart the gusset but no form lay waiting,
   only rills diminuendo, silk
stocking slithered over scallop shelves,
it's down there a flexed-up foot
dangles from the lowest lip
against.

Counterweight
refolds the screen, the screen refolds.
This is the gallant, this the advisor.
   Thick air
cricks her furrowed nape behind little curls I
pluck at,
   so to fold the rays,
   so as to quench,
   so as to thirst.
A clove-studded pomander prickles.
A pheasant raspingly complains.
Sand configures sound-holes.
A dandelion seed unloads
against.

     The plectrum
plays across each stone lip,
lip hollows out the shoe that shapes her foot,
lets the cold wind course and flip
scraps of bast and satin,

cotton insole, runs of buttons,
                    napery puffs out in front,
beaters fan out through the copse,
thumb that strokes the fret
restively, tingling, my finger strums
against.

Δ

Ecstatic legs kick sheathed and silky, moonlight marbles
laths and primed plywood, beams down,
aureate mule! Sip in parts from the
pretty sink, lowest one, the cistern sporting so,
            gurgling with enough and more.
Stomp and float. Dimple. Break out miniature orbs.

This was given me for a present, this kinder-egg cracks.
            Eggshell crazes on shell itself,
            shell itself records shell—
conch lip specifically is roused by a dangled foot
dripping varnish,
the volute lip is sucked by the waves' concatenation re-
glosses that a party scene blathers through,
moonshine stretchers look like shoals of lifeguards
jostle heartily.
                        Tamper-proof pack.

Alkaline as ash earth that breaks, ledge mother of pearl.
No slick talk blanks where what flies substance.
Turn to one side, refill glass, stroll to the balcony,
            comply,
sunrise unrolls its mild coat over a gravel turning circle.

Δ

Smash lamps. Shades run, geese scuttle.
Pandemonium breaks out brittle
boneware extreme cards. Can deference
scrape the wax off this fruit, if so will its

miniature vials stored there, hold juice
and yield it according to terms? Ah the
Antoinettes knew how to show reverence,
but these shepherdesses snap at

waistlines, they are hollow, that applies
to tempting fruit, to their severance
terms too. Behind their nails is building up
dark crud, on fingertips pads of thick film.

Stop pussyfooting, get a grip, pull hard.
Snap the stems. Sweet sap coagulates.

Δ

Viewers log in for their vernissage, uninterrupted tacky
biscuit calendar reclocked.
Terraced echoes channelling their voices, close in-
voluntarily, spring uplift authorised
        rilling through its course,
fills the basin, black is that sunflower rays
are clustering about,
'protogonic but the other side of heaven'.
                    What gives?
A poster-child accepts his flier, a painted ocean
thinks of a scow, a thin batten. They become real ships.

Moonlight sticks in a patch between up-and-down flights.
A generator's hum coats the louvres
        Clear a path. The bower
scuds with wasps, a scalloped seat
of marble wants a gymnast pinned against the tarp
with hard elbows, pert nose,
followed by the spot dragging viscous as an oil drop,
        dangling her inventory.

What will proclaim the lesson, carve out a patch
lit with high definition, there is no reserved side to their
outward looks full of piss and vinegar, agitate
closed protocol.
        Bring the back story to the front
simply by applying heat to its so-stiffened board,
slavers dodge and weave where the bare truth
           ribbons
from a tricorn held out in response and in concealment,
snuffer of the pink.

Δ

Felt fedora flourishes to catch a pink shoe. Hornbeams
shedding bark, such nakedness
I'd never seen, unscratched, unscathed
　　　　she slipped laughing. 'Forth.'
Forth with the fount whose name encircles, forth
but topgallants droop to flapping canvas, water slops
from the viewing point, floods the gallery, an added
　　　　presentation for poor kids.
Bring them forward.
Sift faces peeking through oily smudge.

Be off with you, be off!
Any falling short has to fall forfeit, cloud or foliage,
　　　　confected in advance
seam by seam, passage after passage.
Even to approach freezes what intently is wanted.
Not varnish nor the knacker's cauldron but the syrup
overflows his lip so slowly, it hangs like a curtain.
Gloves and a white evening scarf.
　　　　Carriages crunch gravel,
footmen haste forward with coats, is this one yours.

Cleave the air!
Balsa flies bumpily and skims, clearing dictionary coverts
having brush perused with great O's and M's,
this too finds its course towards the lowest shell's lip:
　　　　　　What gives?
　　　　What turbulates
light behind shaking plosives, propelling wings and
capsules to the graven mottos at their feet, sweeping up
centipedes, reiteratives, the word is
only what her cocked foot kicks to touch, O I
know I had wallowed in the pink: How shall this be?

Δ

      Gummy flux
about a figurine, swirls like a toga. Black maquillage flakes.
O ivory, O stolen
      O ripped bloody
stampede, not a blush,
not so much as dawn's warmth, her pinkish crescents,
lobes sgraffito into chalk,
nostrils pinched or flared—fallen arches, starched sheets—
Let me stoop before this fountain:
      How fleet! How fated! How filmed! How fixed!
How descried!

'Or if my sparkling voice, lower, or higher' rose or fell
          rose or fell,
          did you not suffer
consternation
gasping thirstily: the shoe which flies by day
          flies by day
never caught or dropped—it's a sufferation—
backfilled in its trajectory by back-orderers whose
stylus is parched and Chinese white, a thick deposit no stick
can stir, it has been spied on but cannot be descried
because the words crawl far beneath
seeking just some pool, no matter if reflective or turbid,
for they are but animal machines else,
never near my lip, never itch or stimulate,
mimic, make or mould.

A stony scroll like a bolster for those cupids with its dark
recessive eye socket.

Δ

Let it go. Beauty interrupts the fogs of glassine, rowlocks
creak on the river's stillness and flatness.
                Disconsonance folds.
        How glossily slathering her thigh!
Slick ghosts in ribbons out of oil-bearing shale,
        slide
onto its surface, uneasily at first
seeping from between plates,
curtaining, descending lip to lip down hair-trigger pans
                skirmish and leap in glissandi,
        in a Balinese cascade, ping from the remote
place I am
        telescopically that is
fixed in mud and undergrowth but staring up,

up her multitude, her multi-ply,
        my eye rolling up canvas.
The origin of the world plucks
fibrillating air, that mixture called pure, called clear.
Let it vitrify.
        The swing hangs no set of scales, no reckoning
will best, a ruffle gathers every rill as absorbent
cotton, ribbon flutters tie the empty flying vessel
           pinned to its ellipse
a fold with no pocket, I could hang on those lips forever.

Δ

So cered, as though in memory, so bound, so impasto
slung its hook, dragged it like a hard balloon
in whose volume hardens its lungs as though the spring
makes tufa of the foam, the froth it filters forth.

I bring these shells and scatter them originally.
Each shell smashed incurs its prototype, a hardened cyst.
So the earth clothes itself: that is the shale of self-clothing
eyepieces grub about on, clothes itself with agency,

therefore can take the back and forth, bedded down.
Links you no longer wish to see, sink and this decline
must be her not-thing, I said to all appearances unruffled,
ending on that note. Way overhead flies a shoe's nudity

apple blossom clusters to conceal, its point and sheath,
even as the foot points, pointing it is therefore sheathed;
but a backlash spreads nudity over the linguistic shingle,
slip, a mucous drag, a varnishing. *Le Tic-Toc-Choc.*

Δ

Syllables! Syllables! My heart is in my mouth, I put
her foot in my mouth, my mouth was stopped, not that this
settled anything.
                To be human is a syndrome
and no marker, no, not my tongue can wag that not-dog
contraption,
the homeless arm drags,
eye wanders from its orbit.
I lie in bed amidst the trickles, my candle blows out,
tissue thickens and deposits they compress, they seem no
longer mobile, the be-
longing slips away,
the lung congests, say ah,
what memory, what gives?
           It is the bat slips its fur.
           The flying worm slips its skin.
           The angel sheds its light, it is a baby
balanced on the pan against the folds and corrugations,
holding up
a pink pointed shoe, priapic but a sheath for my eye.

Please give me that leeway, I shall mount it in my stride.
In its stony roll my eye sinks concealed, foliage is billowing
above a plug, a spile,
           undislodged, unaffected sinks my eye,
staving off the flounces, accloying winter
sag and seep down marshy sets and holts,
pressures cloud to keep its formation.
                Syllables will not disperse,
                light not disperse
through rattling stands, nor boughs
shirk the alleviate air they carry.

Δ

               Sloppy dust,
underfoot their shapes merge, could they be faun-like,
gather speed, gain an edge, exaggerated
cheek-bones, smoke-ring haloes
             waft spirally: How shall this be? What gives?
Number them like prisoners on the road.
Seal every spark in amber! Globes bob
on recumbent jets, pans are paved with water lilies,
even the dying sun's reflection skims the rills, cannot sink,
             for it stares into its own steadfast eye
unblinking as dusk promulgates, as limbo fills with
calls this way and that across its marches, with the shrieks
of its shifting populations.

Supposed day
shadows overlap but lunar pull stretches to broad daylight
through the puncture,
swinging to and fro like spotlight's oval or lily pad or like
an eye-patch. Night
and day confuse as in a tangle of dense undergrowth, as in
bramble in that clearing where returning they swing.
Additional stimuli (wind in the trees)
             and prior events
(past experience with predators and wind),
might these send them packing—
             hide
now a tent of winds wherein a foot cannot press the earth
although roots bulge from underneath,
                    shades drive downward. Future machines
burrow up through gashed turf.

Δ

Gleaming scuds across intarsia lids, dots netsuke, splotches
over ebony sticks, ink droppers, variation-free turn-
table bearings, canes
             signing air with bravura, moving
oilily against their counterweights, spring-closing doors
opening such beautiful compartments
                      Come on people, help me out,
'inhabitants of a very varnished green'
                           spring forth accoutred—
I didn't come in regular as regular goes. As previously.

These they clutch: incandescent filament, twisting in its
pearl
neck, brass-capped with screw thread, capsule
filled with argon, or a paper clip
tonguing at its parallels, or velcro
hooks nuzzling into fur, reflective strips
strap her by the ankles securely
             —a C1-synthon headset dips into its cradle, a
spool
now empty dominates a field as though an omphalos
studs its floppiness
                   Help me out.
Propelling fearful stuff, mute and conditional, down the
chute.
                   Extract the dying glow
             to flood the paper
peony, lily. Dry-point children rummage cherry blossom
for what was stolen from them in the first place, fast spoils.

Δ

The shown but unexposed remain opaque and shining, struck
by a sharp flying syllable, nudged by prominent lips,
memory pushed into green capsules, scions echo not
a piercing call/now how extract flutter out of sycamore,

these are but discarded shells chattering beneath naked feet,
percussion that I move by, between stations. Ice-heavy
oak imaginaries clatter. Though old songs are competent,
forest buries them, the forest just goes to show, not a tree

but dies not, but does not, surely I was reeled in on those
ropes and tossed between bright umbrages until shaken out,
those high component joints, my pockets slackening,
replenish me. Wood wasps chew through busily, wiggle into

clouts and congestions, open up, aerate, illume by dint of
bright scuffle, entities can never block their intricate passage,
trumping like with like, like contraries what gives receives,
memory rebuilds in loose-limbed progeny cleaving air

in whatever time they take, the proper time, bursting scent
from laden heads and nodding come-ons, in such patter
breach skin-memory through lips opposed, conventionally
heard in trill or descant, met in dream when stock still.

Δ

Too thick-set this side of things too for what it matters
        cannot disarray the thickets, cruelly
        muss my peruke. Congenitals
will not be singed or hand's flutter bruised,
a flirt machinery teasing boughs
peekaboos.
        Yet nowise interrupts the swell of verdancy.

'The natural world spins in green.' Nothing I get worked
up about or sink a bore-hole or harness waters.
        Moths veneer
        component light, and wings
coat furniture.
Ore-crushing platforms have been quietly
suspended,
                winching gear
behind that brake creaks decoupled in its sabbath.

No more can the charges hold up but they still whisper:
pass the parcel. Tea was plucked brusquely.
Flourished cape shorn
off sheep's back or off shepherd.
        Don't allow to compromise the growth curve.
This picture hanging on our word,
broke from its pediment like a child world
fell from universes,
bids to flourish untroubled while a cast eye orbits.

        Quaint, the constellar map.
Carbon puck ricochets side to side across a slippery rink.
        A frictionless scarring. Searing cold.

Δ

Don't shovel it, thick dapple, cap, cap, cap.
Depth of texture swells fanfares from concealed flat panels.
More even than what gave birth, hunted or
       sunken with all hands
       worked clay,
light diffusing from a dead bulb plays across scrim
deposited as frost,
light breaks from isolation through scrim
daubed on an ensemble pit.
       They have the props.
       Lit layer on layer.
       They can be lavish, hurry off
twitching bone, but leave the body clay to palely glow
behind armoured glass thickening with algae.
           Help heave my carcass out.
Pull me up onto the soft ridge with some adhering soil.
That's on the way to eggshell, nothing völkisch,
fighting shy of glassily transfigured, pearl.

A dragon lunges for a flaming pearl
scratched in monochrome, a thousand years have not dulled
lustre, the bed
can be identified, but light
pearls the flaw
         spectral concrete/
please I must concentrate please I might diffuse/
Would standing on firm ground bruise my heel
as across an upturned dial
content with themselves they walk,
       pink scintilla bursts,
its capsule plummets on thrilled air turning no blind eye.
The earthen floor years layer, shears surface,
       catkins and winged seed,
'for she her sex under this strange purport did hide'.

Δ

Winged foot that has borne me thus far, pah!
Further to the tip of interrogation, further
where stone wings web infant shoulders,
canvas baby shoe mocks a pedestal's exalting.

Take your last card from the shoe. What you
see cannot swarm more gently than the
site guides its arrow. Fingers are mussing fur,
this one pips me at the post, the marquetry

instructor dumps his tray, a doubtful footing
slides into the cut where slippery cards
compete to look unanimous. They succeed,
because the dispenser ticks one up one under,

ticks one again with a juddering pertinacity.
The self-cascade scatters seed at its base.
Folded wings fail to unstick. The closed pool
tars thirstily, shingled with a single word. Ah.

TORNADA

Fire breathes fire over tacky lips to shift
Les Ombres Errantes
for motionless the clouds err.
Formations belie themselves
vitrified, they blush, sort of.
A cloud-harped pillow-block, a celadon
stoneware flanks out.
There is no elephant in this room
flat truth comprises.
Where once shifted images, DP or A
or B&D,
before firing
characters were cut in body clay.
There were those pottery
and stone had moulded their skulls.
There were those
Our heads depressing feathers, heavily
squeeze air.
Does not a bird make.
Fire breathes on racked lips.
Four notches in the rim exactly
signify lotus leaf.
A see-through slip makes audible
lalling rills
interlaced, interpolated, built.

Raising votive cleats,
they beat the bounds of the special
class of objects, stir,
cleaving tight bark, probing spongy
crumbled base. Optical or co-ax,
crumbled meat
deputies crowd the figure,
lips swell a stack of plates,
single use plates

wattled, one on one,
supervisors chew over fortified.
There were those
wielding little mallets, march! you
maillotins, beat out the hours.
There were those
burrowed into ripe fruit, resort to
paper palaces, what stacked up
if on paper
blew away. Stipulations,
bubble packs, air
vent hammered down flush.

What shadow falls.
What shadow is rotating.
Bird lifts off salamander coping.
Shadow cuts a deep disk
through the ply, the layers of super-
imposition,
folds one on one, wrenches them like
bread, like books like a roof.
Similar to paste
cloud hangs a blimp, hangs fire.
The ash pit stirs to let fly
its first groped word like a crocus,
chance thereof.
Heaps start to churn.
Should pivots switch
counterclockwise, and this airy island
hover, throwing shadows
like the span-master, world-stretcher
etched on his wheel.
He stopped for a single glove.
The shoe tumbled.
Because the wheel turns
characters blur.
In its shadow brightness

participant, every tongue lipped.
Whose the cries, whose the breakers?

Not for long did they play freely,
soon were docked.
Now they shake back
characteristical number.
There were those swing
out of view, intercept a high-kicking
leaf-fall
dripping tight as celery. Such zephyrs,
such bold specimens of
cabinet high gloss. Language
lumps for their heads, pulse emission,
these wanted not centres
all the same.
There were holdouts
gave thunder credence,
blood pooling on a waxed mild shelf
delivered down
humming rails. Exposed
racks of seconds,
final touches to a page of shadow,
rays anointing the head.
Glaze wants a lighter nuance,
firing *sang de boeuf*, sicklies over
imperfections.
These were the stirrings
of a new genus.
Then even to conceive outside
dissolves in nightmarish din.

What gives.
What threw off suckers
batten on the skin-tight, the slippery
dismantled earth,
tucking in amidst

ground object-logged/
logged
with the given and fortuitously dropped.
This one makes no sense.
Deposit it in crossed beds.

*One by one I pluck the bowl off its trivet and this is a production
line. One by one I break the bowl and on the trivet there is no
bowl so far as I make out. When my tongs reach in where no
bowl seems to be, they clasp the bowl, withdraw it, and it is a set
of song-bowls. This can be repeated with a flushing cistern; it
passes the falsifiability test, it rings true. Remove the bowl one by
one, and the continuous gurgle, the flutter, how will you remove
these, that, what exactly? The void shakes and sends its emis-
sary. Keep your eye on the ping-pong ball which one by one leaps
across a trampoline of water, so symmetrical it must be empty,
but the ball is jumping on a body of water, on a full expanse.
When I say I pluck the bowl off its trivet, it then says a nothing
doing, it is a saying, no more—still, the bowl resounds from that
saying so, one by one and shatters, then its emissary goes out and
it is I who say this from the void, from the fiery void.*

The light framed like tents ladders.
The tents were erected opposite.

What shadow falls.
What shadow is rotating.
That had been reckoned post-obit.
Razor-sharp leaves
cut down to the pith with characters
felt the cobalt hoods
fall across their logograms,
thought themselves caught, spindrift
blowing on the parterre.
What had tampered, chafed
the whole contingent
before it could be sorted and named,

what pitted brass and hung
portentously, cutting loose
like down an orchestral chute
music dins and blares,
compacted for storage
in bedrock or at bedside.
Water shakes.
These contiguous blocks vibrate.
Glass cracks, bowls sing
fantastical union.
Then pollinate, inflict their
thumbnail shoots like a lily
beats the clock,
no wonder circles and semicircles
crawl with numbers, ossify
like cenotaphs to the future.
There they go. Bound to
lunge for advantage. Must
have been tolerance in that chord.
No rules broken.

A chaffinch drops down the
smoke-hole, losing feathers,
take that for an omen.
One figure gathered up
near the portal,
teeters back and forth,
hands stretch to rip
the ensign from its valiant staff.
Smog-red maps are populated
long foreseen.
Don't tug so hard, push-button
eyes or modern touch design,
index to a lash
flutters to be laid up.
Chipped in its neck with details,
fast to learn, staple it.

The hammer drops, the master
strikes the blank.
A name. A signature.
The very form discovered,
wherefore pink gout obstacle/
leashed love
pendulum, it twitches sadly,
impulse
creamed off in a Doppler shift:
its jerk-off ceremony must end, where is
the meal, where is the cloth spread out
for destitute, hidden onlookers,
the snagless competitors?

The pole shook out its ribbons.
The criteria stayed quite robust.
On the first level, shops.
On the second level, shops.
On the third level, shops.

Jack sprung and Jill sprung
forward in one leap or back
sniffing on a tussock, embryos
thumbed from their gold
packs, the writ runs genetically
wakeful ahead of hounds.
Look behind over the lake,
its once ad lib
ridges in formation.
Abeyant they are fixed,
fixed until explosive force
springs them
at whose flanks they wait
in glassy standing waves: Vagrant
draughts
afflict the horsemen,
what's still wanting bruising

plunges in ash and lime,
a cup bangs down a well.
Listen how the horn winds.
Why leave a broom abandoned
stage front?
Listen for its tallyho.
That's a fateful cantilever,
that's a sharp scent of fear,
nothing budges but the shadow
foreshadowed.
Carefree tap the brink
shadows dance towards, horizon
flapping distantly
stretched across the beacons.
Flames leap from towers
beyond peaceful vineyards.

*Bread then is shovelled from the oven, not to be shared out and
eaten but to be tapped, appreciated, sniffed, then this loaf's image
to be stored in memory. This bread communicates, that is, it serves
competitive purposes, but by so serving loses all heft. This is the
loaf its index. The loaf one by one registers the variance of the loaf,
keyed to proving time, bake temperature and length of bake, use of
steam. So then how to represent the loaf in full? The heel and
crumb, the cottage loaf, the tin, but not as these constituents or
types? Without recourse to the thrice-baked rusk or Eucharistic
mysticism? Must I see myself see myself? What is dawning? What
is dawning? What is dawning? Where is the table where a question
must be answered with a full mouth?*

Then design a full mouth,
one on one disbarred,
self-cancelled stroke.
Ramped
scalar sheet, scalar moonlight sheet
trembles and a plaintive birdsong
loops the horizon,

keeping out intruders.
Do not bituminous treasures tread.
Butterflied and pounded.
Three-inch golden lotus
simpering across wire, boneless
dives into a hutch,
there were those
pressed by callipers, see
hieroglyphics,
confluence of waters.

What judgement falls.
What judgement is rotating.
It did not lose its compass but lost
grip on saturated ground,
sentient fallout.
Lay down the head
pinched at base, still malleable.
There was a moaning.
There was a crawl to heave
themselves to windows. These
though were flat inspection plates
transparent to themselves,
transparent slip,
allowing what they see gloss
overlooked, no more thicken.
Cups bake echoed on their trivets,
blushing all over.
Praise to the chiasmata
every time a fast forward
where the break itself breaks, roots
postform,
smoke is but its own preview.
Few have had a foresight.
Cerebrospinal fluid. Break to
fields of broken crockery.
As though grout itself builds.

Great dedicators make a diagram,
smash it repeatedly.
Moreover, more,
eyes flicker, tongues lisp
conversation galante. Birds catapulting
parallel to what the dream
slingshot apparatus.
Things of this nature simply pass.
Had you disowned parts weigh.
Where once lines rose and fell
were cicatrized.
Your neck its deposition.
Lay down your weary head.
Put your head the frame the frame
locks telluric, echolocated.
Tell-tale moon
angled to its gear, ready-greased
locks on above the sleeve.
No play, no wobble.
There were those so thought.
There were those lips swelled
salts of silver.
Bulimic fountain roiled with cupids
syncopated swimming.
Flocks assumpt themselves.
Each bird lifted off, *l'oiseau frivole*.
Day in day out.
       Stop
Day in day out.
One on one.

It's the flat truth.
Drovers watch their herds
slaughtered, red poll.
Notable a slab of divination.
Householders cool their heels in yards.
Stratagems of cloud

stole the foreground, what glass.
Pierrot brushed his cheeks with
ash not chalk,
foretold in string figures.
Here is a tree unprecedented
gives shade.
We stretch ourselves out at last,
ply our flatware, eat
off blank plates, cut our cloth
according to the frame.
Fire begins to smoulder.
The ghost devours much bar the head.
It means thorns.
Every single single singled out,
one on one.
Suppose the pink bat flies
through a body of light.

RECKITT'S BLUE

Geese squalling shriek tight and wheel   , spiel
Their signature, perform their splash,

Stretch across the muscle that the sky tenses and
Relaxes then pulls in   Outriders.

War canoes disperse through inlets on the systole
          Over   tight waves

Tense nets gather   These were the drafts,
Turmoiling,   these block

In the compelled   unities
Reproduced in this or that fog,

We are open,   open, we are open. Rostrum
Greedily furrows   oar drags,

Thrust to the rim of space with no buoyancy, feel
Leaden, if it did dissimulate it might

Join   grubbing out geodes, or who lays
          marsh on the granite shield,

Not to break loose but to see the far-flung straggle
Thousandfold across the inlet.

What is the septum   dream? We are en-
Ruptured in glass. Twine and leather

Hardly twitch to perform   Pin feathers,
These alive   catch our drift

Latch on as if emotions while   on freeways,
Float our houses built as vistas—look,

Kitchen needs a fishhook, bedroom   a canoe,
Bathroom blood that it be cleansed,

In the foyer raiding parties gather, round the boiler
Steam   .

Come now you foragers and shred   , gouge
Hunks   , off you scurry;

Dip and flap to scour those lawns sun sinks before,
Peeled back to polished bone,

Amplify   to dissolve the shored-up banks,
Like tide in a delta bulges at crossover.

When gods were young, waves broke stupidly,
The moon wanting merely that.
Let cancel cancel cancel passage,
Term crash: he curves unseated
In fissured air, he first wounds itself,

Snagging holes its ritual   ,
At games, at canoe regatta,
Maybe so but never fret,
Nor   at the break   dumb lacquer
Sun bestows: water cuts and opens,

Hooks shilly-shally   ,
Punched cards or pit divisions,
Stroke follows stroke across the board, tongue
                    breakers roll in vast fettle,

Deliver   posturing little gods.
Mere shadows have voracious   spathe
Bodies whistling store—in that smooth
Piano black, a spirit board   .

My house's windows are bricked up.
Shell cracks to the fairer prospect. So it is said.

Their sampler would cast
Crow feathers, beetles' backs, nubs of black corn
Harnessed over water.
Crust of sky staggered down, line sculled.

Balance double curve slew rate
Purposive but gawkily offbeat,
Hailed firmly in coordinated flight-path eastward.
Slap   chair, mouth   mail
Offerings like gab grain.

Likewise cable-fed with millet, near-kin or bound
If remotely
Fretwork of soft soot
Freshly fallen, turns its mirror back,
            measurement enrapturing

What spirit guards you our forever body
Hoarded. Lapping
Surfaces the points drain and lines constrict
Where spuriae were prone to belly,   raw clay

Fledglings soon will break
Towards the grain elevator. Say is it said parallel.

Flutter must be brought   wings angled,
Clamped to their shoulders, set on course.
Swept across the board
Controlling warp so the   withers,

Limber sway foretellings sealed now at both ends,
thus fork,   interdict, oppose.
High coin rings authentic, rings gold, under-
Pins aberrant stars: Channel 5, Channel 6,
Forced into reeds
Like pharaonic children flicker across bloodlines.

Spathe axe   , straw locks,
     stone ripens   matting ties.
Reeds bristle at the estuary absorbing ill
Degraded soot   cut with blood shows tracks

Swooping down to sample   one shines,
Another channel opens
     blood from one previous,
This makes one white and shining of countenance.

I obstruct and bubble
Down Laurentian granite, webbing. So saying skip.

Soul gathers, more more more abruptness
   plies   ,
                  puts it on while strong lobed drag
Growls and resists. Man overboard.
Funnel. Make a paste of soot blood slakes,

Else clapped elbows, clapped knees
In-filled the gap
                           trip lash a sampler
To his grading stick, then rile him good   ,
Scarify his plump cheeks, balsa
Dugouts itching to maraud

Fitted GPS truncates
At iron tables in clearings hacked for the purpose.
Felled trees, feathers of the cut wing
Tressing a so sought-after   pleat follows pleat

                  finger-stalls fly the channels!
A complete head rears above the prow in
Its preview of annihilation, scar plan.

I look out for sharp edges, univalent.
I am caught, I am snatched, I am snapped, spoken.

Staggering through the blockhouse suppose waves
Not soon enough. Casket   with soot holes
Woven between   Top-notch
                                 Bark
Shutters need a loaded card to run up.

I swipe I swipe I swipe. Bogus
Blood-group,   vaccinations torrent,
Credit rating and a took throat. Organs dissolve
In 24 hours.   shrunk booth shots,
Each image bleaches spirit calming measures—

If the shape of the river bed changes can the water
Rill as it once did?
     hear the telling rush under the thin hull,
How can it follow
                    islands will be submerged?

Heart and lungs underneath peg,
Slap outside the blockhouse fronts the great river
Trickles but its still-strong
Translucent warriors glowing like blue jellyfish,
Launched to ingest missing parts already outlined.

Supplies needed   . Nut trees unclip their loads,
Produce floats availably. Go. Clusters
Rise higher, reddening
With intercalated trash, glowing softly soot.

As shrunken discs remount
Masks to steal their souls.
Low the confounded tap
Keel, shone bones rattle boards like thimbles

Slop mercurial noise traders ratchet, mark,
                , clap the board
Noisily. Clump yield of that kind hard to pass up.
When sun slips moorings,

Things full of themselves shrug off its lustre.
Booming sounds
Beneath the threshold, piss stench,
Need re-seating,
Soot sets the compass, soot carrying the day
Drumless shall sustain clamour. Sun ascends.

As would its counterpart.
It is the portent of what was said already pouched.

Now how shall   measure swell or
    treetops' curvature, fresh
      salt waters   . Also   satin-
Wood, palladium, floated in to catalyse the fumes.

Though flat   the captive
Head against its oblong board, yet tide
Surges through, held calls sluice
From the bursting navel, beetle lacquer drips
Inflame opposed surfaces. I mortice, I

Hung in thick cotton threads,   straining hawser
Hauls,   , a wrenching noise
Fleshes out story boards
Dragged to their birth squat; desolate   join—

The too-devoutly counted trickle
From between knees, synovial flow
Catches light in treeing an impacted   ,
          divided pulls together. Red plates clash,
Peals and changes shake the rookery:

I throw away the wrapper and disperse
Like beech-mast crackles where no creature pads.

Each a bubble-wrap panoply,   composite
Of poses How to stomach that,
Whistles for the downwind, avaunts
Snap head bobbing up, spurned—

Knuckled by a harsh sun, a   split
Trepans them like subjects bear its heft,
A fluxionist, collapser of this
          if sunken shines along rifts.

Star walls lower. Nights are cordoned off.
Unavenged dead loiter against copper ductwork.
Drumming won't entice
Who were born to dance and flit,
Floaters on earth
Teasing and promiscuous, it counts if a socket

Winks from a distant body,
Warm   against the dash, trail wires,
Charge up   , densifying   surplus,
Bone the wood shank the sun smacks.

He was attached
Just above the opening, wearing my false sex-mat.

In the outhouse in the straw what goes ahead.
On the enamel lip what goes ahead.
Behind the missing door what   . Emblem
Of covert hopes all know all belong
In twisted hair, a dreadlock, the growling.
Produce the sample. Engineer   conditions.
Bury in the taro patch
Beneath   . Upholstered settle.
Crush on the iron frame string bits
        debasement a greasy slide.
The buttockless stared.
The sealed men's house stood atop its thin poles.
Keys, stamps, mobile phones.
Lumber in the pericardium a pin number accesses,
Neutralising bad thoughts, flicker
Kapkap that rotates on   panels, filigree
Openwork, men with bloodshot eyes, we women
Map their path with soot and blood.
O dark clouds the conch calls,
I shall stunt myself down to the neck so earth blurt.

Water glasses in and glass waters like an eye glasses over
To outstare   : so waters rush down the glassy eye

Rolls behind the lustre it apportions, the eyes' armada
Bristling with quivers-full, ruddying like time-lapse orbits,

Tethered like the floats marking contours of a sand shelf,
Rotaries that saw   across the big suction pads,

Dredge into the mooring, steal fishing rights, exact water
Options that boom under the fretful high buzz   :

Where once were carved screens, chancel walls, our house
Extraverts, inside glosses out and nothing is glossed over
But incisively broken, neatly parsed, picked apart with ultra
Precision tools then displayed in clear suspension, listed
Organs are sectioned, the roving eye performs its autopsy,
Heart confirms, wildcat operators square off flats of mud
Shaken so to slop out wells, mesh will let the catch tumble,
These are their spoils. Sluiced all dissipate where island
Purses, cowries, heat-bonded pockets, floored eyes follow
Strung skulls turning in a tuned flood, each a self quadrant.

Box the sample, calibrate   the spring flood,
See the ceiling grind slowly,   ground stump

            so unseal the catacomb of seed,   run
Without a lock, its on-line activation protocol

Frigate birds reject the pallid sprouts, a foul-smelling mat
                that lawn is but death's waterfront,

The trade group daubed in white will disembark,
Agents of the tribe retrofit a blank display with hoardings,

Highlight   walrus tusk and cans of tuna. Headless,
Neckless, shoulderless, surveyors click the bundled sticks

Fanned across their backs, feel towards a spirit trap, stray
Where nerveless   spirit scraped out

          stinging particles, stormy light plumps the veins,
Vibrates a diastolic harp of vines, slit gong   dithers

          coating lemurs folded in volcanic clefts,
Sunlight scarce applies its thought while ash sighs airborne,

Sifted through   microns-deep, these deposited
In light-controlled drift gloss   , blink of an eye

               from saturation to   alluvial.
For detail see miniature skull exploded in vitro and labelled.

So in darkness   cancellations ridge beneath finger-pads
In closure   corrugations buckle where serpents thrash
In skin-tight   patinations transfer between the surfaces
In approach   supplied reflections writhe in anticipation
In congress   fur stops words behind the mouth, its ket
In volutes   electrical the poor ghosts in their element
In the wave function   , in monsoon blast
Blades of air conditioned chill, knife   a bumpy surface
In   flotillas, feel the bumps, enfilade on ocean swells

Islands racked with cries soaked   off cliffs,
Intifada   , cries the dead reply to with their own cries
Interrupting waves, forming swells known as *dunung*, shift
        , staggering the files of shod creatures walking
Through hell's yards: Neatly docketed
They tow their   line through dense slabs of algae,
In their heads   they cannot echo, cannot
In their lucid trance   pass along a scream,
In their calm smooth frictionless   usal

Brought to this pass   this chiliastic dead-end, human
In their peering eyes rolled back in a scoured, sanded cast.

Behind the illuminated exit sign a cataract churns on a loop.
By the emergency stairs a symmetric frenzy shuts its trap.

Before this 'I' took she floated lazily,
Land lay ridged in waxberries and heather. Striped
Bass was good, sea sucking shingle, all good,
Acting as she   used to. She unpacked.
Huffed and puffed but then caught the breeze.

Wrasse were rainbow-fresh. Another time,
        under the belt.
Look there are ritual spoons, hung like trophies,
Hung like the ready tongues that wag,

This one for the forceful river
Tells or tills the current, cleave, riddle, cleave,
It wants to cram stuff and substance back within.
This other countenances,
Gently allowing smoke to figure.

Let its curls tighten, wreathe as blue organs
Bunch like the knots of muscle
Air is proficient
In convulsing to arouse life altogether flat.
Breaking surface in a house they embrace landpipe:
It would look as if I thought I wanted freight.

Soon the tight-wad obstructs the road ahead
                    . Greaves clamped on her shins,
String bag between her legs,
                    cassowary hooks
Weave the underbrush, kokorra dream-eyes

Promontory shapes   flitting
Disembodied, blinking out.
Low   whirring   creosote
Alighting among sharps,   black pouch
Pulses
Clustering about a shuddering and mighty sponsor.

Then left the keys dangling in her trunk   as if
Sensate details ferreting her spine,
The wattled   plus   the sumptuous
Sought to shrink, air
Performs with feather thrash, waves
Perform where island eruptions dimple currents.
Stiff custard   sap and pith.

How shall I pass the indeterminate
Varieties of figures, wheat initials, spathe tongues.

Plight that plies   feathers fan no farther off,
Stunted   slew of bubbles.
Night-time freezing does it. Hard
Rain   bulkheads
On sets across the claim yard, rain as fixed
In channels as   a slew of bubbles

Etched as though indelibly lines up
Under the overhang.
Purposing to show her by such a method,
Trickle-talk under the board. Play this by ear,
Play this through the swells and finesse on target.

Inside shutters wait unspoken blank skies.
She had to   .
If the advanced one should
Wander home, she finds   but a furred

Saucer, vacant mould squatted in already
        brutish organism
Intact
            Green viscous plume of its own.
This was   going to happen.
I gurgled me. Beset thus by the senses apt to take.

Be it   sky schemes then it blanks.
          Call this lodging
Where mats open.   One bleaches on the prow
Nudging in amidst glassy swells,
Rippling out and repulsed, wheeling
If and when   board-fellows

Square things up
Between the deluge and upsurge. Globes of weed

Bloom   into reachlessness,
There's a copy   traipse sky
Gulls scream and drop into. That seeing
Scaled back, that hearing it
Ran diagnostic: its   involution
Agonising, mordant, burrowed in, enfolded

Among the shades   , a nacreous paste
          out of cloud and soot clutch. Must
Green   with vivid poisonous frogs,
Flatten on the marshes, network
Masts   , restricted by a set ceiling
Over distracted earth rollicking they make tracks.

Shure this is no trix   forgary so sheathes
                    or shining permeates,
Girt inside the bound to follow, bound
Sunlight checking   one after
Gaseous globes. Drift until
               canopy
        Heart and lung aerate pulp
Bubble-wrap ripped open. Snatches then weighs

Objects from the hand-list indited.
Indeed no-one posts a sign where animated floats
Sway their objects   —
Glass slings sway below   , lock step
Forward on blue combers'
Slow approaches, woven spathe boulders.

          That designing devil, she who
Shouldering her load, pounds sago
Day in day out, sings a closed
But too restive song   , white-
Shod above breakers, nonetheless a
Tutelary spirit filling bark beaten for a sail.

A flint stays in the fist, and fire   it's going
Way over. Amber keeps its viral store.
On deck the pyxis moulded to the binnacle
Contains seeds. Some are sealed with resin,
Some lead-weighted.
Yet still the prow holds course, it will go way over.
Only the shielded exercise   .
The world lies mute and bandaged, wickerwork
Performs   long-soaked,
She lies in purple buzzed by bees. When standing
Scrunches glass floats, when standing breaks nets,
Her hand shatters early air, cascades
              smithereen and celebrate her mien,
Birds fly way over.
Give her a break she will lift it,   the water
Booming below, mist
Includes itself,   opaque,
Have a heart I say and the sun lifts in its envelope
Glaringly hidden—give me your arm,
And the fetch of the wayward tide thick with slime.

Behind glass the smooth ones   no leasehold
In their skin soft as soot,

Generally shrug off   , generally sustain
A flat high surface, yellow pollen

Winks on no stamen, blots of pollen star   skin
To a force figure referent—

But gases writhe   each incomparable
Like moulded plastic

          each evacuates the mould beyond thought
Felt as pure invitation,

Undefiled, unruffled, necessitates light's   trigger
To set off its colour-shift,

Spiralling cinereous, a yellow-dusted   , promissory
Anthers. Its figure full to bursting,

          tune in grey to red, yet one slouches to the lip
              too addled to log on:

A pouch   in his living chest, tuned to obstruct
Signals with small stones and herbs,

Inset but it claims no height, depth or quality: either is
Caramelised in the sump,

Or else the lath no frequency can hollow or dislodge,
No two ways about it, scum

Substantially   . Us we stare at ostensibles en-
Raptured, like with pink salt

Decrepitate the mind. Decrepitate the body. Meteors
Of phosphor   spatter,

Cannot serve to steer,   back outside the inlet,
Bump by bump down a thigh I carry,

Bump after bump, sequent   currents stagger-
Weave, intervolve between islands

          firmly on one pressure point and it springs open
Like a visor swivels for its pledge,

Whatever is released   , it goes viral
In the most   flail,

We are open we are open we are open, stars squawk,
We are the truth, the light.

Without forgetfulness these crowd the present cohort,
Ocean stops in salt starry ridges.

And the aneurysm burst in   abruptness.
Pacing salt boards, a gong
Moon was fracturing   . Thrashing
In her pouch with hooks and matted fibres
Whether meat or textile, was she through? No.

Unexampled   on the last day of closing,
          flump worldly goods
Board and batten   company
Withstood them all. Trades are on hold.
Who saw this through? No one.   look into it.

Sealed   bulkheads over
Quietly slide across to choose and be chosen.
Shut it.   Biotic stray
Surges and buckles, hotspots ease a population
Through   at eye-level tight smiles

          vacantly where water pools and feathers
Ruff, the ears fill with her chant, I feel lumps
                    insect swarms
Bulge in my palms and hang from my feet,
Having been bold to plot her aortic frequencies.

proceeded from the great united. Clots
Flew from cavities. Such were the emblems
Palmed blockhouse walls,
Moons smash against   case of negligence.
Brands. What-you-wish. Canoe
Ribs are broken,   boards sold openly.

After the desecrated course each picks his teeth
With much more caution.
What of its nature does that impartial orb conceal?
Thews grip the wall. Cordage
Of hypserpa: spreads them all out
Drying on the trestles.
Clear as was the swerve that knocked
               cassowary headdress,
Notice every spur had both sex organs.

So put another arm   , so was broken, so
Caught what came flying. Such were fringes
Stray plants colonise. Vines
Obscure   , fibreboard
Thickens at the touch stamped at once across it.

Were that coast   , designed by its slippage,
Taint after taint, to touch,
              drawn starkly, although stars
Winnow out and separate, taking thought
Down,   shoreline masts blink answering—

Too much dwelt upon,   distil
Twigs dusk gathers,
Repeated words emulsify and clot,
Green churn.   Lumps fill the breast hole
          and by these lumps we navigate,
Tree after tree sets roots among them.

Pink stars dot the pale resumed
Thought sky.   his feathers
For his pains. Winter cherry in its mortice
Languages. If stars squander
                prick out but efface,
Peremptorily bandage.   Crossing waveforms
Ramify and bulge. He was blue when hauled up,

Frost burns and stars tip bare songless twigs,
Specify a trough which I wander.

It is the closed thing I want that it stay closed,
That flightless feathers fail they stay furled.
Nor want fitfully drive magnetic skirl
On polished surfaces home like a beacon.
Snap then the embrace and fling the dust
Of affection that it convolute in lesions
Kaleidoscopically opening, now would I drop.

Entities will not ingratiate, nor in other words
Put out proxy labels, every joint unturned
Has been stripped from their high-gloss
Fecklessness. My cheeks stay rough, unrazed
By knife-edge fishtail vents. Appraised
The parts shake back to the place at first
This that mapping no parts corresponds to,

Their bulges do not mass to the apogee, nor
Aspire to anything of that sort: as glaucous
Pods liquid-filled have no lips to distort,
Disconcertingly like Canada from the air
Spreads a coverlet of bubble-wrap, tugs
At its pockmarks, arranging these split
Hairs and oxbows like nematode blind turns.

It is the closed thing was a fresh blinded eye,
Whose nerveless tackle dropped supplies
It could not right or invert or make stucco
Intramural decor. A dissonance between
Tears and wax stood out sharply, keen
Blades coupling to the striped muscle.
Here is the arc I short and short for I must.

Some found their métier here like Gauguins
Of faked-up ceremonies, chewing plans
Over in their lampless parlours, slots
Kept empty for their dumbshow guests,
Temporarily adjusted. There were stinging

Sensory detectors, no replica could seem
Comprehensive. How doth a city sit solitary,

Lacking correspondence between sectors,
Circular motifs run narrow hollow tendons
Poorly clocked. It is the closed thing I want,
Small raised structure houses finials for
Dummy runs, slicing versus crushing, decor
Caps churn ocean but I lamp out from
The entitled box with my lightweight spear.

Thus a part foreseen was soon made clear.
Mandatory to view those daily rushes
Before diving, deep in Sepik river swamps
Aestheticised, slashed and burnt, a fright
Served up in video. Props men swarmed
Around the lamp one T-beam supports,
But silently: the power supply interrupts,

It judders like a cistern replenishes its gut
With yes/no denizens, their dazzle stripes
Swimming through the commons unfussed,
No sooner green ripens than green breaks
Opportunely, it contrives a variant Us
From famous chaotic lozenges and dots
Streaming towards the puffed-up cumulus—

Copyist because this cloud topography,
On/off phosphorescent cells, blips of solder
Sealing cubicles, grids of shrunken heads,
Issues in a charge that when expressed
Through oily mousse, electroplates and
Glosses over bodiless, forms out of ditches
Lift but parts are flashing simple switches

Flaring on the lapsed sky in running stitches,
Scheming and flipping. Triple siren sequel

Taps at the impervious toughened glass,
Shaken in harmonics war-canoeists bump,
Scattered through a cloudy green sheen
Plaited by stone outcrops, but whose swells
Bear four directional sticks or tuning forks,

Whose loud swelling song is raised above
Shuddering agreement, the sun's sulphur
Shimmer bowls. Moreover algal bloom floats
On Mekong, Mamberamo delta, passionate
Slit-gong missives prod through openings
The islets and the line spread, their clatter
Breaks up the manifest, and criss-crosses.

He hath hedged me about the deep boomed,
And through catenaries of watchful spume
Sends his eye. Presided over by that orb,
Infiltrators flicker with their thin bodies
Tense and attuned. The visual cache shrunk.
What I embraced was but a smooth trunk
Devoid of any reach or means to absorb.

How I dreamt the organism! How I dreamt
Gathering! Relics some fret over, new buds
Ossified, bronze booties, what were these
But blocks, the trophies of stability. Croaks
On bankside, buzzing grass, a stick break
Brought together swept in a voltaic surge,
Upspringing now crescendo, and a fervent

Mouth with blue strings like washing soda
Puckers for encaustic inlays that in gashes
Travel out. So pull tight the tourniquet.
Where did eyesight start from but evicted
Legs to clabber swamps that burn or chill:
No longer able to absorb such injuries
They splinter, work loose, engage and crank,

Except a bent spindle was the crank, what
Re-stimulates the outflow for a soil bank,
The seed bank, the stick stirring up a storm,
Booms are lowered into rifts that squirm
With disorientated fish. Along their ridges
Crawl patrols in formation, rhythmless.
It is the closed thing I want that it stay furled

Like carbon filters, tight-packed corrugation
Locking bud to body, phloem to a forest,
Thrown in the logarithmic points, polarity
Of sand, raise voices rather than adjust
Time, space, effusive light, like props
For carbon suits. Pleats trickle insect dust,
Tar consolidates and steady heat composes

Substance from foam and disdained scrub,
It stands to reason rudimentary tails flick
Their bounden entities scuttling into shadow,
Matted there in green slabs. Ex-post-vito
Blocks the exit: then air will inspissate
Life sentences, flutter-tongued and stopped—
Blurt it out where tapioca pearls clumped:

The throttle makes the note, stricture bursts
Convulsively, 'twas summer and a brave
Shout squashed the worm conventicle, dust
Reception jack, the unifying capsule which
Of mud consists. Recapitulating mud. Into
These the outer world sinks, datagloves
Transmit its aftermath to stock death trove.

Dead feathers choke a stealth raiding party.
Pilotless the jet rakes and banks, stretch-
Throated, full-throttle interlaced cassowary
Scream shivers, then high turbulence
Despatches them, stripping off their cover.

It is the closed thing I want that it stay furled
Clamped down and surging: it is their musick

Near close enough.

ROUNDABOUT

Trumpet-blower. Own trumpet-blower.
                    Huh
Haul away.

.

At the roundabout why
look in the rear-view   a bunch
sways all juicy-like.
At the island, sea lanes interrupt,
sprig pinned   .
Waves become chaotic, promised
        showcase. But in the rear-
    bunch torrent
never more postpones.
Lorries spill loads.
Smash-and-grab,   through
phosphorescent shoals, a star-
punched into the plate all bloody-like,
spawns ones
                order that goes,
a hook lowered, while its block
    bulb sets

manifests in the form of a lizard.

.

Hauliers whose lined-up bone
    the making of them, blue yellow
sheets in shadow monolith,
blue yellow
doings
—air   hiss—
        hauliers clutch sandwich

lath for signposts, soon   beset
bridges sway.
Sheets of bleached
pith hang from buttress roots,
hammered   blink or not
                    storms,
            breaks lumpish
tail-backs,   despumates with yellow
            taint,
why do the men,
wrapped in whitening smacks
shake the whitening hand.
Get   in   , booms shudder.
        links litter boundless sand.
Vegging out   serrated
            bluing yellow white,
hauliers on break riffle   ,
ply rubber thimbles,

turn   up their object armada.

.

The swell had made pronouncement.

Dagger spines broke. Put up
disowned trumpet

        fft . . fft . . .

Rolled across the truck plaza. Ears had
pounded, then   lurched inside,
stuck his wad like that.

Is someone here about to see to me?
slicked in phosphorescence.

Mould creeps along the margin,
is that   , foaming at the mouth

      fft . . fft . . .

RECKITT'S BLUE

Blue

Synonym, variant or common name

The English firm of Reckitt & Sons produced the laundry product Reckitt's blue from 1852, which was originally a combination of synthetic ultramarine and sodium hydrogen carbonate (sodium bicarbonate). Use of Reckitt's blue and other laundry blueings is documented in a number of ethnographic contexts such as artefacts from Papua New Guinea [...] and Australian rock art [...].

Pigment Compendium: *A Dictionary and Optical Microscopy of Historic Pigments*. Edited by Nicholas Eastaugh, Valentine Walsh, Tracey Chaplin and Ruth Siddall. Oxford: Butterworth-Heinemann, 2008.